WOODWORKING

FOR BEGINNERS

**STEP-BY-STEP GUIDE TO LEARN THE BEST
TECHNIQUES, TOOLS, SAFETY PRECAUTIONS
AND TIPS TO START YOUR FIRST PROJECTS.
DIY WOODWORKING PROJECTS WITH
ILLUSTRATIONS AND MUCH MORE!**

TOM FOSTER

TABLE OF CONTENT

INTRODUCTION

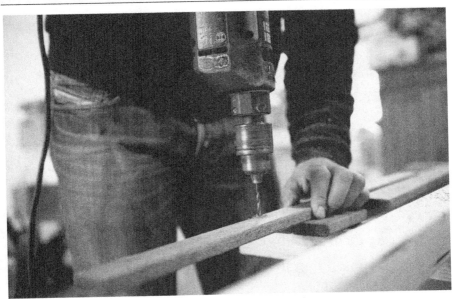

Woodworking is an activity that has been in existence throughout human civilization. The best thing about this activity is that you don't have to do it on full time basis. You can always do it on part time and hence engage in other economic activities.

Once you learn how to build wooden items, you can build an outstanding gift for someone special in your life. You don't have to buy an expensive gift for your spouse or a friend. You can decide to make something special for them and hence make them feel important and appreciated.

You can also use your woodworking skills to make some money by commercializing the venture. For instance, you can start making furniture and then sell the furniture at a profit. You can also start the business of carving wood as per the client's specifications.

Do it as a hobby. Woodworking is one of the most exciting hobbies as it will keep you busy and help you put your imagination into something useful. On top of that, it is a cheap and fun-full hobby.

Do you know that you can totally transform your home and increase its aesthetic value using wooden products? You just have to know how to make wood products and you'll be set to go. For instance, you can build a unique dining table that will totally transform the home's interior décor. You can also make a chopping board that'll amaze your friends once they set their eyes on it for the first time.

Researchers from across the world estimate that it takes less than 10 seconds for someone you just met to have a first impression of you. If you're thinking of expanding your business and closing in more clients, you must add a personal touch to your office. To do that, just build a unique and attractive piece of furniture and then place it in your office table. Once a new client enters your office, they'll have a good impression of you and hence increase chances of closing a deal. After all, what kind of person would refuse to sign a deal with a unique, organized and neat person? The piece of furniture will portray you as a very organized, focused and neat person.

Have you ever thought of owning a unique piece of furniture; something that can't be found elsewhere. Well, to distinguish yourself from all your friends, peers and colleagues, you can decide to make something using wood. For instance, you can carve an effigy of yourself or your pet.

What will you do if you buy a 42 inch television while the biggest wall unit in the market can accommodate a 24 inch TV? No need to worry. You can always build the wall unit if you have the skills to do it. With woodworking skills, you can build something that isn't readily available in the market.

Buying quality furniture is quite expensive and may drain your finances. Even though you'll use more time, it's cheaper to build than to buy furniture. You should therefore consider building instead of buying furniture.

Once you have woodworking skills, you won't ever have to seek the services of a carpenter to repair broken furniture. You can always repair the broken furniture by replacing the broken part or repairing it.

You don't have to buy plastic furniture when you can't afford wooden furniture. Wooden furniture is more attractive and makes a home or office to look more natural. One more disadvantage of plastic products is that they are not durable. Once you learn woodworking, you can always build home or office furniture.

Woodworking skills will also make you proud and increase your self-esteem. You'll feel so much better if you can point at a piece of furniture in your home and tell your visitor that you're the one who built it.

THE BASICS OF WOODWORKING

Woodwork means a lot, but here's a relatively simple description that most hobbyists are likely to support.

Woodworking is a productive craft that requires wood to be cut, shaped, and fitted to create beautiful and useful things. Woodwork is nothing physically demanding, and you can build at your own pace. The basic concepts are simple to learn, but it is always a hobby that is new and challenging as the skills grow. When you love to solve problems, you love woodworking. I have been at that for over 40 years, and with each project I create, I face new challenges. This is part of the process. It's also worth making cool things for your home with your hands and brain. In general, woodworking is an incredibly lonely experience: you will enjoy woodworking if you are a little introverted and like to take on tasks from start to finish.

Who are the workmen? WHO are they?

There used to be two woodworkers ' myths.

The cranky shop-teacher who taught kids who didn't want to be there a truly boring lesson, and the elderly grandfather who put in his garage a long time to build a birdhouse.

Luckily, these myths are not valid anymore. Woodworking now has more diversity than ever before, thanks to the affordability of tools and materials.

In the last ten years, two groups of people have been making woodwork a hobby.

Women first.

First. It wasn't long ago when a woodworker woman was unusual. Woodworkers are now commonplace women. There's nothing someone can't do with woodworking.

The second substantial demographic increase was between the ages of twenty and thirty. I still meet people who work in the Silicon Valley or have some form of office work and feel the need to do something with their hands.

What is the difference betting to a "builder" and a "workman?"

A manufacturer is a relatively new term that has emerged in the last decade or so. It's an all-round term for people who like to work in various crafts. Ultimately, we are all manufacturers.

A woodworker is a producer who is mostly interested in learning to make things out of the wood and grinding them. Sometimes we bring in other materials, but the focus is on wood. It's an inexpensive, timeless material with which you can quickly build.

What is the difference between wildlife and woodworking?

It's a bit vague, but I tend to think of carpenters as constructing houses and buildings — building work. I don't find making a house as woodworking out of posts, beams, and 2x4s. Woodworking tends to be the construction of furniture and other moving objects. That said, many call woodworkers carpenters, so that's not significant.

What is the Difference between Cupboard and Furniture Making?

Again, there's no active line between these two terms, but cabinetmakers create permanently installed products, such as your cooking cabinets, and mostly deal with the visible surfaces.

Furniture can be placed anywhere the owner likes, and more pieces of the finished piece can, therefore, be seen.

The cabinets could use more than most mobilizations of plate wood and are supported by screws and other mechanical attachments, while the furniture also uses solid wood and is assembled in general with stronger carpentry and glue. The production of furniture can require higher precision.

There's a lot of overlap here, though. I've designed tons of furniture with furniture and screws and saw impressive cabinets that compete with high-end furniture.

Woodworking Types

You may have an idea of what woodworking entails, but there are a few ways to approach this art.

Hand Tool Woodworking

In the last 20 years, woodworking hand tools have had an immense revival. Woodworkers use hand tools to build items using traditional tools and methods. Handsaws, chisels, scrapers, and planes are preferable than anything that fits into a wall.

Hand tool workers probably feel more connected than any other form of woodworker to the process. You need patience, and you have a longer learning curve; you build it slower and much quieter. Nonetheless, personal satisfaction and satisfaction can be immense.

Power Tool Woodworking

Power tools such as miter saws, table saws, sanders, and boxes are omnipresent and can be an inexpensive way to start construction projects immediately. The cutting of a board on a tableau takes no part in the skill and finesse of using a handsaw.

The biggest downside of using power tools is that they can cause serious injuries. It is nothing that should keep you from using them, but you have to learn about safety procedures.

Virtual Woodworking

Virtual technologies have been everywhere for a while, but in recent years they have become more affordable and attract more and more hobbyists. The primary tool here is the CNC machine that uses a router to cut precisely on flat pieces of wood. You need to layout and design your entire work on a computer, and the device takes care of the rest and cuts all your pieces out. When it is cutting, you don't even have to be in the same place.

A laser cutter or engraver is the other tool in which hobbyists invest. This tool enables you to make even more accurate cuts than a CNC and produce some beautiful art. The most significant drawbacks are the costs of using digital presses. You can spend enough dollars on them quickly. They are small, and you probably want a table saw and other power tools in your store. Many people feel that digital tools make them less "connected" to their woodwork, and they are happy to do things hand in hand.

Blended Woodworking

Many people in their shops have a combination of hand tools and power tools. For example, a mixed woodwork method can make most cuts with a table saw, but a chisel can be used to cut dovetails by hand. Many people think that hand tools have higher accuracy and power to cut technical joints and enjoy improving their expertise in these tasks.

Specialty Woodworking

Two types of the woodwork are specialized in by enthusiasts, usually artists. Scrolling and woodturning.

Woodturning means making cups, spindles, and other rounded projects with a lath. It's like carving clay with wood and chisels on a potter's wheel. The only real downside is that the lathes can be quite costly.

In a typical woodworking shop, you can indeed find uses for both devices, maybe you need to occasionally make legging tablets or add some decorative scrollwork to a fantastic bookcase, but usually, they are not tools that you use much.

Fire Round Rapid! Is It Dangerous, Woodworking?

Probably safer than walking, but not as reliable as wood. Understand how the tools work and how they can be appropriately used — using common sense.

Indeed, why do you love wondrous works?

Woodworking is fun, and you can make cool things for your home, but ultimately it's all about figuring out who we are and finding out that life can offer so many more inherent benefits if we take time. Unplug a few hours a week and plug into some power tools.

Woodworking is portrayed in many ancient Egyptian paintings, and a considerable amount of old Egyptian furniture has been found in tombs (such as stools, benches, tables, beds, chests). The inner coffins found in the graves were made of wood as well. Woodworking is not about perfection but fun and development. Woodworking is a potentially dangerous hobby. Most hand tools are very sharp, and when misused, power tools can cause serious injury, even death.

This type of project suits the school exhibit very well. Students will not only enjoy selecting their glass or mirror inserts and making the finished product but also seeing how passers-by are impressed by their item.

In your woodworking shop, tools aren't the only potential danger. You need to think of your respiratory system, too. Tools with the same shape and depth of the curve will have the same number as Sheffield, no matter how full or how long the shaft will be. The higher the number of sweeps, the more angled the blade is.

Jigs are used in cuts or hole drilling to increase accuracy. These are used to coordinate a series of repetitive cuts, so there is no need for frequent resetting of devices or pieces of work. Woodworking jigs help to increase the overall amount of time spent on a project.

A Look at Wood Working World

Looking to Start a New Hobby? Scrapbooking, photography, and painting are just a few hooked peopled hobbies. There's one hobby, though, that was launched well before those three came along. That hobby which has attracted quite a lot of attention and an excellent investment for those who started it a long time ago is woodworking.

Which, instead, does woodwork include? First, let me explain the fundamentals of woodcraft briefly. Understanding what your tools are is a vital part of wood carving. There's a whole variety of tools in woodwork, and it's not just limited to your hands. Know your devices, and never underestimate each other's characteristics. Know then that more than three types of wood are used to create random wooden crafts. Just as critical as searching for woodworking projects and learning about its methods is also understanding what kind of wood you are going to be using. If you're a novice, then it's only reasonable for you to use the softwood type, so you don't need to use complicated cutting hand tools.

When it comes to woodworking, the possibilities are endless, and the significant part is that the imagination is at work. Not only are you able to save money, but this hobby also harnesses the potential to be a great company.

It takes a little bit of creativity and commitment to create a woodworking project, but it's enjoyable. Once you hold the complete product in your pocket, you will know the effort valued it. And the more you repetition, the better it will become for your work.

It is possible to learn how to make stuff out of wood by just having an idea and start, but if you can get some instruction, it is much simpler. Most people get this help by going to the local community college to take a lesson. Others are more autonomous and are searching for career strategies that they can work on at their own pace independently. Several of those professionally designed plans are available on the internet.

STARTER TOOLKIT

Once you decide to pursue woodworking, the first priority should be getting all the tools you will need. In most cases, you will already have most of the basic tools right in your home. However, it would still be a good idea to purchase some more pieces of equipment. You might also want to replace some old tools in your toolbox to be sure you have a good set before working.

In any case, there are two broad categories of tools to be familiar with: hand tools and power tools. We will look at each category, as well as some of essential tools to have from each. We will also take a look as some of the miscellaneous items that you can include in your shop tool chest.

HAND TOOLS

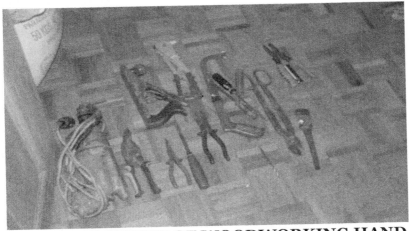

AN ASSORTMENT OF WOODWORKING HAND TOOLS

Hand tools are the easiest to get when starting woodwork, as they are often readily available in the home and are inexpensive. Below are some of the essential hand tools that a basic woodworking kit should be comprised of.

1. Hammer

The claw hammer is perhaps the most recognizable of all woodworking tools. It not only lets you drive nails into wood pieces but also remove them using the clawed end. The clawed end also serves as a counterweight to keep the hammerhead balanced. It can also come in handy for a variety of other tasks.

Weight is an important consideration when purchasing hammers. A heavier head would mean a stronger force for every stroke of the hammer, which makes driving a nail easier. However, it might also prove a bit more difficult to control. Another important consideration when purchasing a hammer is the handle size: the longer the handle, the faster you can swing the hammer, increasing force. The most preferred weight for a claw hammer is around 450 grams.

2. Hand saw

The hand saw is another hand tool that is almost universally associated with woodworking. And even with the advent of power tools like the jig saw and the circular saw, many experienced woodworkers find it a must to have at least two different hand saws included in their toolset.

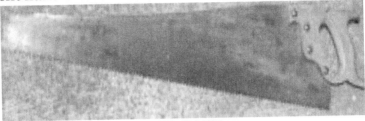

RIP SAW

CROSSCUT SAW

While there are several different types of hand saws, the two essential kinds to have in a starter kit are the rip saw and the crosscut saw. The main difference between these two saws is how they cut into the wood: the ripsaw cuts along the grain while the crosscut cuts across the grain. Also, note that the number of teeth (denoted as teeth per inch/tpi) determines which saw should be used for cutting a particular size of wood stock. Saws with higher tpi are suited for smaller stock while a lower tpi is useful for doing more aggressive cuts on larger ones.

In case you don't want to have to deal with two separate tools, you can opt to get a saw with interchangeable blades.

3. Tape Measure

A RETRACTABLE TAPE MEASURE

Accuracy is crucial when working on a wood project, as you want each piece to be exact to the specified dimensions to ensure correct fit. Here, a tape measure would be more preferred than a ruler, as it is a lot more compact and can be easily carried around where needed. A 25-foot retractable tape measure will be ideal, as anything longer than that can cause the retract mechanism to not work properly.

When buying your tape measure, it is important to check the sturdiness of the hook at the end. When this hook becomes loose, it can slightly slide out of place, which can throw your measurements by as much as an eighth of an inch, which can screw up the accuracy a lot. Also, don't let the tape roll back too hard, so as not to damage the tab.

4. Screwdriver

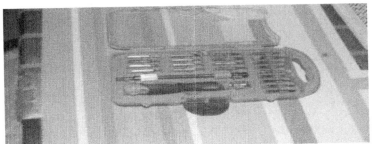

Screwdriver set with interchangeable bits. The bits are the common sizes for general use.

Screws are useful when you want to easily disassemble joined pieces. However, they can be quite a pain in the neck when you down have the right sized screwdriver for the job. A good screwdriver set should come with the most common sizes for Philips and flat-head screws. Though less common, it would also be helpful to have some star drivers and Torx drivers for these types.

5. Chisel

The chisel is probably one of the more overlooked of the basic hand tools, as it is more often associated with wood carving. However, the chisel can actually be a versatile piece, as it can

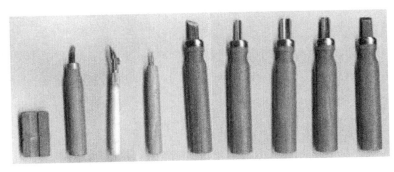

be used as clean out joints and saw cuts. Furthermore, it can be used for such novel tasks as prying two joined pieces from each other.

A COLLECTION OF WOODWORKING CHISELS

When buying chisels, it would be a good idea to grab several different sizes. Choose ones that are made from high-carbon alloy steel or chromium-vanadium alloy steel, as these will resist wear and tear much longer. Also get those that have hardwood grips with metal caps on the ends, since this can take hammer strikes well.

6. Hand Plane

BLOCK PLANE

While the hand plane is sometimes overlooked by beginners, it is one of the essential tools that a woodworking starter kit should have, as it is used not only for smoothing wood but also for shaping it according to needs and trimming it to meet measurements. A block plane is a good starting plane for novices. You will probably be surprised to know that getting older block planes is actually a good idea, as the quality of the steel used for the parts is often higher.

POWER TOOLS

Power tools are designed to get common woodworking tasks done a lot quicker and easier. These tools come in two different varieties: corded tools, where you need to plug them to a power outlet, and cordless tools that have their own battery pack. Almost all power tools come packed with an assortment of attachments, letting them do the work of several different tools.

1. Circular Saw

While the circular saw is sometimes considered to be more of a

carpentry tool, it has also become indispensable for the woodworker's craft. The circular saw lets the woodworker do cuts that can be saw. It can also be made to cut accurately by using clamps to hold the piece, which is ideal for dealing with plywood or fiberboard.

As is with the hand saw, the number of teeth is important when getting a circular saw and saw blade. A blade with more teeth in it produces finer cuts, which is ideal for making accurate slices.

2. Jig saw

Cutting curves into wood pieces is often a difficult task to

accomplish when using regular saws. A jig saw makes the work easier by giving you better control to guide the direction of the cut. One feature you would want to get with a jig saw is orbital action. Unlike standard jig saws, which simply move the blade up and down, orbital action jig saws angle the blade forward driving it into the wood in the upswing to produce a smoother cut. Do keep in mind that this feature is usually more common in pricier units, but you still find it

3. Table Saw

For many beginners, the table saw would be their first major acquisition for the shop. As it is where much of the work will be centered. A table saw lets you cut large pieces of wood, as well as accurately trim smaller pieces to size. Many table saws also come with components that let you cut varying thickness of wood at desired angles.

4. Power Drill

Going from cutting, drilling holes will be another common task you will encounter. Here, you will probably be surprised to know that a corded power drill will be a better recommendation than a cordless one. This is mainly because corded drills are less expensive and will be able to provide constant power much longer.

5. Router

The router is a versatile power tool that beginners will find handy for a variety of tasks. A stationary model is a good option for beginners, as it will get most tasks done easily. Choose a unit that is at least 2 HP up, which has enough power to handle larger bits.

6. Random Orbital Sander

RANDOM ORBITAL SANDER WITH SANDING DISKS

Of all the woodworking tasks, sanding is definitely one of the most laborious, as you will likely be spending hours to achieve the desired smoothness of the wood surface. The random orbital sander makes this task less tedious while freeing your hands from all the pain of having to vigorously rub sandpaper onto the wood. Another great thing about the random orbital sander is that it lessens the appearance of noticeable sanding marks, as it moves in a random motion instead of a definite pattern.

Miscellaneous Tools and Items

Apart from the above tools, there are several other items you should have in your shop's tool chest. These items will come in handy for a variety of tasks, and can also be used when you need some improvised tools.

1. Clamps

Clamps are arguably some of the most indispensable must haves around the shop. Their uses range from holding glued pieces firmly together while the glue sets, to holding pieces being cut, to securing wood beam being bent into shape. Clamps come in a wide variety of types, including bar clamps, spring clamps, face clamps, corner clamps, and C clamps.

2. Pliers

While pliers are more commonly associated with electric and electronic work, they also have a ton of uses around the shop. Just like clamps, pliers can be used to hold wood pieces when working. Pliers can also be used as a makeshift wrench to loosen bolts on wood panels, as well as a lever for prying wood pieces.

3. Levels

When making items like tables and cabinets, it is vital that they stand flat on the ground. A level is useful in checking whether this is indeed the case. A basic level has a small clear cylinder filled with a liquid and with a bubble suspended within.

4. Speed Square and Builder's Square

A speed square is a tool to let the woodworker determine whether pieces that need to be at right angles with each other are indeed such. At its most basic, the speed square is essentially just an L-shaped ruler.

5. Marking Tools

The two most common marking tools that you should stock up in the workshop are the chalk and the carpenter's pencil. The chalk is your everyday variety that can be readily bought from school supplies stores.

6. Work Stands

Work stands are particularly useful for those who have to deal with small spaces. These can be used to hold the tools you are using so that they are not lying around. Work stands can also be very handy if you need to transfer from one room to another, as you can simply prop them anywhere you need to.

7. Air Compressor

Most of the power tools you probably own are electrically powered. However, there are some run by compressed air, such as pneumatic nail guns. However, air compressors are a lot more useful than just powering pneumatic tools, as they can be used to run other equipment.

8. Vacuum Cleaner

One thing to remember when doing woodwork is that it is going to be very dusty. Thus, you need a handy vacuum cleaner to clean up after work. However, regular vacuum cleaners are not designed to deal with a large amount of sawdust.

BASIC WOODWORKING TECHNIQUES

Woodworking can be challenging for people who are just starting this hobby. However, you will learn new skills over time. We will discuss about the different tips and techniques that you need to know about woodworking.

JOINERY TECHNIQUES

A good woodworker is able to do seamless joinery. Joinery is the process of joining pieces together to form the final product. It often refers to connecting woodworking joints. We will discuss about joinery techniques that you can use for your woodworking projects.

Joints can either make or break the project. It is important to take note that the more difficult the joint you use, the stronger the finished product is. Below are the types of joints woodworkers can use to create their different projects.

Type of Joint	Description	Illustration
Butt joint	This is a simple method of joining two pieces of wood at the corner or from both edges. However, this type of joint is not strong, but it can be reinforced by using glue, screw or nails.	
Dado joint:	The dado joint is often used in joining bookshelves. This joint is characterized of making a cut on one wood to receive the end of the other.	

Dowel joint	The dowel joint is done by drilling aligning holes in each piece of wood. The two woods are then glued together in order to form a tight joint. This technique is tricky as it requires a centering tool to align everything in place.	
Lap joint	A lap joint is similar to the butt joint, but a rabbet is cut in one wood so that the two pieces will overlap. To secure the wood in place, using a screw, nail and glue can tighten the joints.	
Miter joint	This joint is made by sawing both ends of the wood that will be connected to an angle of 45 degrees. It demands accurate cutting and measurement of the angle to create a steady and straight final product.	
Mortise and tenon joint	The mortise and tenon joint is a traditional joint that has been used by many woodworkers since time immemorial. It is a strong joint that is made stronger by adding a peg.	
Through dovetail joint	The dovetail joint is valued for its aesthetics and strength. It requires patience and accuracy to cut the interlocking joints. However, the joint itself provides a strong visual style on the project.	
Tongue and groove joint	This type of joint allows wood shrinkage. It is commonly used on wood that tends to shrink over time. To make this joint, cut a grove at the edge of one piece of wood. On the other wood, cut a tongue that will fit on the groove.	
Biscuit joint	A biscuit joint uses a biscuit joiner that cuts oval slots in the mating work pieces so that they can be glued tightly.	

'ING TECHNIQUES

allows you to set the glue as it dries. It also prevents

structure from moving while the glue is setting. Below are clamping techniques that you can try to secure the glue in place is it dries.

Technique	Description	Illustration
Securing odd shapes with heavy bags	You can improvise clamping your woodwork by using a heavy bag of lead or sand. This will save you a lot of money when buying expensive clamps that can hold odd-shaped wood pieces.	
Use long bar clamps when clamping carcase	If you are gluing a carcase, the best way to do it is to use long bar clamps so the carcase is suspended.	
Use tapered blocks to clamp sloped sides	You can make tapered blocks from ¾" scrap wood blocks. Make sure that it is 2" wider and 1" longer than the height of the item that needs to be clamped. You can use the tapered blocks to clamp items that have sloping surfaces.	
Use felt pads to protect the surface of the woodwork	Clamping can cause problems like scratches and nicks on the surface of the woodwork. To protect the woodwork, make sure that you put felt pads (self-adhesive ones) on the clamps so that it will serve as protective pads on the furniture.	
Use clothespin to clamp tiny details	When gluing small pieces of wood or stock, using a conventional clamp can be difficult because they exert too much pressure that may break the woodwork. Instead, improvise by using a clothespin to clamp tiny details together.	

MEASURING AND MARKING TECHNIQUES

Woodworking requires anyone to be able to do proper measuring and marking on the wood. In fact, the success of a project largely depends on your precision to make the necessary measurements. Below are the measuring and marking rules that you need to know in woodworking.

If you are going to make measurements that are less than 1 inch, it is important that you use a rigid metal ruler. A tape measure flexes so the measurement that you will make might not be accurate.

Always use the same tape measure throughout the construction of your project. The problem with using different tape measures is that there might be discrepancies in the graduations of the measurements.

When cutting the wood to length, be sure to square one end before you make the mark. This is to ensure that you don't make any mistakes with the measurements.

The riveted end on the tape measure can cause inaccuracy in the measurement over time. So, avoid using the riveted end and line up the 1" mark with the square end of the work piece.

Use a mechanical pencil for all marking tasks as this leaves a fine narrow line that does not leave any doubts on where you need to cut. You can also use a lead pencil but make sure that it is sharp.

Use a square to mark your wood pieces for the length. You can have a straight mark that is perpendicular to the edge of the blade.

FINISHING TIPS AND TECHNIQUES

The right finishing that you use for your wood pieces can make or break the finished product. It is therefore important that you arm yourself with valuable information on how to create the best finishes for your woodworking projects.

Surface coatings: Surface coatings provide clear finish. They also provide added protection to the wood. Examples of surface coatings include varnish, lacquer and shellac.

Pigmented finishes: Pigmented finishes are not transparent and they look like paint. Examples of pigmented finishes include black lacquer. They also exist in natural finishes, so they mimic the color of natural wood.

Penetrating finishes: As the name implies, penetrating finishes penetrate the wood grain instead of set on the surface thus it leaves a very natural look. It also provides low luster on wood.

On the other hand, below are the techniques that you can use to add the finishes on your work pieces.

Waxing: Waxing is a great technique that you can use to add finish to your wood. It is labor intensive, but it provides extra protection to the wood. Waxing can also be used to rejuvenate old finishes on wood. Although labor intensive, it does not require too much maintenance. Waxing can be applied over the penetrating finish.

Staining: Staining is used to improve the natural color of the wood. This creates uniformity in the wood. This is especially great if the wood has inconsistent appearance.

Glazing and toning: Glazing and toning are two techniques that is used to provide highlights to the wood as well as improve the color depth of the wood. These two techniques are also used to add an aged look to the wood.

Pickling and liming: Pickling and liming are two types of traditional finishing that are used in accentuating the grain of the wood. This is achieved by using two different (contrasting) colors which include the base color and another color that is rubbed into the grain.

Bleaching: This technique is used to lighten the color of the wood or remove any discoloration brought about by the presence of moisture. However, it is important to take note that this process cannot remove dyes and stains.

Distressing: This technique is used to give aged look and texture to the wood. It can be done by sanding the finish after it has been dried or rubbing a chemical solvent to remove some of the paint.

WOODWORKING STRATEGIES

HOW TO SQUARE ROUGH CUT LUMBER ON A TABLE SAW

If you get rough cut lumber or mill your own logs, you will need to know how to square them up. Here is how to square them on a table saw. First you will need to make a jig though.

You will need:

8 1/2" x 48" thin hardboard (if you plan on doing a lot of boards longer than about 6 ft. long, do 96" long hardboard and 1x3 below)

1x3x48 strip of wood

3-5 toggle clamps

Measuring tape

1) Put glue on one face of the 1x3 board and align it parallel with the long edge of the hardboard (smooth side down) and clamp them together until they are dry.
2) Attach the toggle clamps to the top of the 1x3 so they can clamp a board to the hardboard.
3) Place your rough-cut lumber on the jig so that one of the rough edges faces out over the hardboard. Clamp it down and measure the shallowest spot from the 1x3 out. Set your table saw appropriately so that it will cut off all the bark the entire board.

4) Run the board and jig through the blade with the 1x3 up against the fence.

5) Remove the board from the jig, and measure the slimmest part of the board again, this time from the new straight edge out. Set your fence appropriately and run the board through.

6) You now have a squared board and can now use it on the miter saw for a reliable cut.

HOW TO EDGE BAND PLYWOOD

If you plan on making cabinets, Murphy beds, or anything with veneered plywood, you will need to know how to finish the edges of the pieces before you assemble them. This is only for edges that will be seen, so you can mock assemble it without fasteners to figure out which edges need to be finished. Once you know which pieces need banding set them aside.

You will need:

Pre-glued edge banding (one that correlates with the wood species veneered on the plywood)

Double or Single Veneer Edge Trimmer

An iron

Small smooth block of wood

Scissors

Bench Clamp

Sanding block (120 grit paper)

1) Cut a bit of banding an inch or two longer than the edge it's being applied to.

2) Place the panel in a fixed bench clamp with the edge facing up.

3) With the iron in one hand and the veneer strip in the other, start ironing the strip onto the edge. The heat warms up the glue and then sticks to the edge. Be careful and steady though, the glue will melt and stick but it will stay warm for a few minutes and can easily be picked up or moved. Also, if this happens, simply re-heat the glue up and peel the banding up and start over with a fresh piece.

4) Once the entire strip of banding is applied to the edge, quickly grab the block of wood and press the glue into the banding and plywood. This will seal the bond tightly. If needed for longer boards, lead the wood block with the iron to warm up the glue again.

5) Let the glue cool while you trim the ends of the strip flush with the end of the plywood with the scissors.

6) Next, take your single or double veneer edge trimmer and run it along the length of the board, trimming off the extra banding.

7) The banding should be the exact size of the edge it's glued to now, but it might be a little rough. Take your sanding block with 120 grit sandpaper and gently sand all the edges smooth to prevent splinters and cuts. If there is any glue residue that oozed out onto the wood, try to sand it off as best as you can. This is an important step especially if you are planning on staining this project. The glue will prevent the stain from soaking into the wood and it will look bad.

8) If you have multiple edges on the same board to band, simply rotate the board and start all over again.

CROSSCUTTING VS. RIPPING ON A TABLE SAW

When you rip boards on a table saw, you are pushing them through the blade and the grain pattern and the blade are both going the same direction. They are parallel. This makes the effort needed to push the board through a lot easier since there is no resistance. Crosscutting a board on a table saw means you are pushing the board through the blade, but the grain pattern is perpendicular to the blade. Often times, you are crosscutting boards or plywood that are too big to be cut on the miter saw. Usually having a second person help you crosscut is the best tactic to take. One person can keep the board square with the fence and hold the end that hangs off the machine while the other person pushes the board through the blade in an even manner.

Quick Overview of the Types of Joinery

Joinery is where you tell the difference between a good woodworker and a DIY-er. Some techniques are easier than others and some are more decorative while others are more utilitarian. A good technique to learn for traditional joinery is the Lock Joint. It's a good way to make drawers since they hold tight during movement.

You will need:

Two 3/4" thick scrap boards (having two different colored boards would be best as they can be easily distinguished during the learning process)

Table Saw with a Dado blade set 1/4" thick and a normal wood blade

1) Set the table saw up with a 1/4" thick dado. Raise the blade 1/4" up and 1/4" away from the fence.

2) Crosscut the first board at this setting. This would be considered the drawer side.

3) Set the blade height to 3/4" tall. Then for the 'drawer front' stand the second board vertically so that the butt of the board will be pushed through the blade.

4) Next, change the dado set out for a normal blade then set the blade height to 3/8" tall. Move the fence 1/2" from the outside of the blade (instead of the usual inside of the

blade). Lay the 'drawer front' down with the fresh cut end up against the fence and send it through.

5) Combine your boards and you have a Lock Joint.

Other common types of joinery look like this:

BRIEF LOOK AT THE DIFFERENT SPECIES OF WOOD

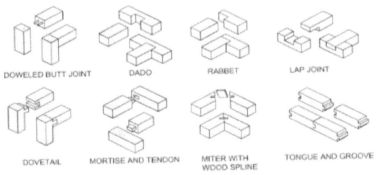

DOWELED BUTT JOINT   DADO   RABBET   LAP JOINT

DOVETAIL   MORTISE AND TENDON   MITER WITH WOOD SPLINE   TONGUE AND GROOVE

Here is a sample of some of the different species of wood. There are many more, but these are the most common for woodworking. Take a closer look at the grain pattern, distinctive colorings, knots, and other unique features of the samples. Keep in mind, these samples have a few coats of clear finish on them. Raw lumber tends to be more faded.

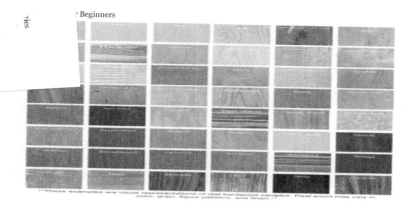

Notice the difference between White Maple, Curly Maple, and the Birdseye Maple. They aren't different species of trees; in fact, they are all Maple, but certain environmental conditions have given them these unique and sought-after effects. Only about 1% of the Maple logs are high quality enough to be labeled Birdseye or Curly.

These figure patterns become more pronounced with how you process the log as well. The least expensive cut, flat sawn, has the least amount of work and waste. The miller cuts the log in flat slabs and you won't get any unique markings in the grain. Quarter sawn gives the wood some beautiful figuring though. For this type, the log is cut from the center out. Rift sawn is the most expensive technique to purchase. The miller cuts the logs like the spokes on a bicycle wheel, from the center at an angle (between 35 degrees and 65 degrees) outwards. You won't see many rift sawn boards in stock at the lumber mill, but you can always special order them that way.

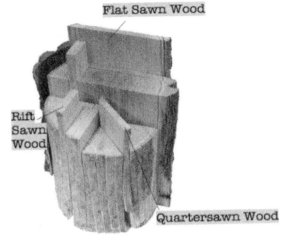

Pine, oak, birch, cedar, poplar, maple, hickory, cherry, walnut, and mahogany are the common types of lumber you can find in almost any lumber or woodworking store. The other woods in the table are more exotic and often have to be special ordered.

They are more expensive, but they are also usually more stable. Start by working with domestic lumbers until your skills grow, then take the leap and spend the big bucks on the exotic lumbers for a project. You will not be disappointed with the end product and by then you will have less of a chance of screwing up a piece and having to buy more. But if you do make a mistake, especially on an exotic wood, keep it around because you can always make something else out of it like cutting boards, knife handles, carvings, or even wood mosaics.

DIFFERENT TYPES OF WOOD:

Hardwood vs Softwood

The two major categories in which the woods can be split into are hardwood and softwood but beware, do not get be fooled by the names. Hardwood is not always hard and the softwood is not always soft. The trees having flowers and leaves usually have hardwood whereas coniferous (with needles) evergreen plants are softwoods. The cost of hardwood is more than the softwood most probably due to its availability. Investment in hardwood is worthwhile if you need a solid piece of furniture like a bed or dining table etc. If you need some intricate or carved wooden article to enhance the look of your living room, you can go for the softwood without any hesitation.

HARDWOODS
Oak

Oak is one of the most used woods for furniture and is known for having more than 60 species grown in US. It can be divided into two types Red or black oak and white oak. White oak has grayish brown color while red oak has the reddish cast. White oak is considered to be much expensive as compared to the red one.

Properties

It is used for solid furniture due to its strength and beautiful grain. Its coarse texture and prominent grain are due to the fact that large conductive vessels are laid in summers rather than later. You may see clear medullar rays or streaks in quarter-sawed oak lumber.

Uses

It is mostly used to craft English and American country designs. It is famous for reproducing Gothic and William and Mary or numerous transitional pieces.

Cherry

It is considered to be an expensive wood and is available in the eastern half of the US. It is valuable and you cannot use hand tools for it. You can also call it fruitwood. You may like some antique furniture pieces made of cherry that still look new even after years. It may turn to richer red or brown with time.

Properties

The color of cherry varies from light to dark reddish brown and can be accentuated by adding a stain to it. It can be used for making cabinets and furniture. Its closed grain characteristic makes it easy to polish and do not need a filler. You can be innovative by mixing cherry wood furniture to any other wood as it has a property of complementing any other woodwork at your home.

Uses

It is famous to be used to craft 18th century style furniture. Cherry solids and veneer are also commonly used for the French and Colonial designs. The different uses make it quite versatile.

Mahogany

There are many species and grades of mahogany depending upon where it being grown. Honduras Mahogany is indigenous to Africa, South America and Central America. The price depends upon the quality of Mahogany. The African logs are thought to be of lesser quality while a log from Caribbean is known for its quality, hardness and strength. Philippians mahogany can be easily purchased at a cheap rate because it is not that beautiful and durable although the color is same.

Properties

The color of mahogany varies from medium brown to deep red brown. It has a distinctive grain and uniform pore structure. It displays ripple, stripe, rope, and ribbon-like appearance. It finishes well and considered to be an excellent carving wood.

Uses

It is widely used in Victorian style furniture or crafting of contemporary furniture.

Maple

Maple has 115 species out of which only 5 are found in US and grown commercially. It is resistant to moisture which makes it durable than any other wood.

Properties

It is the hardest timber and is expensive due to its strength. It is used even in the bowling alley floors as it is resistant to shocks. It has even fine pores giving it a smooth texture and grain. Grain is sometimes wavy, curly and leaf-like figures. It is light brown in color and can endure paint and stains.

Uses

It is used for making the back of violins and like for its patterns. Maple is used for butcher blocks and is dense enough to be handled by power tools only. Bedroom furniture of Maple that you wish to use for long will be a better decision. In early 1990's

American colonial furniture was made of Maple extensively and now is considered as antique.

Walnut

Walnut is the most famous and versatile wood and is found in Asia, America and Europe. Whenever you are going to buy fine furniture, you will look for walnut wood. It was used traditionally but is still in demand. Its color is usually light to dark brown with purple streaks in it. European and American walnut have their unique characteristics.

Properties

Furniture made of walnut wood is light weight but quite durable and strong. It has an attractive grain in it and it takes finishes very well. It is used for making cabinets. European walnut is considered to be the "King of Kings". It's slightly light in color as compared to American black walnut and has a fine texture. Its wide range of application makes it the most popular and worth experiencing. Figures like crotches, stripes, curls, burls and mottles.

Uses

Walnut was used in cabinet making particularly in 18th century.

Teak

It is another expensive wood available in yellowish golden shade to dark brown with light and dark streaks. It is found in Southeast Asia but is grown in Africa as well.

Properties and Uses

It can be used for veneer or solid pieces. It's strong, heavy and durable. It has a distinctive, straight grain. You may like it for doors or flooring purpose. Natural oil is exuded from teak that makes it bear different weather conditions resisting decay and cracking. Oriental style furniture was made of teak.

Rosewood

This beautiful timber is known for its fine quality, fragrant nature and close grained property. You will appreciate its color that ranges from dark brown to dark purple with prominent black streaks. It is quite valuable and looks great when used in manufacturing of musical instruments like piano casing, furniture, veneers and art projects. It is difficult to shape with hand tools.

Sycamore

Its resistance to splitting makes it favorite for the butcher blocks. Its pinkish to reddish brown color and moderate price makes it a good choice if you do not need very costly furniture. Hand tools are suitable for Sycamore.

Basswood

Another inexpensive, common hardwood is Basswood. It has even and straight grain. It is pleasant to eyes when used in combination with rare woods like Mahogany and Walnut. It has an attractive color ranging between shades of creamy white to creamy brown. It has small pores and is close grained.

Ash

Ash is another moderately priced wood used for making furniture that needs some bending. Although there are 16 species being grown in the eastern United States, but white ash is most commercially used type. It is a hardwood that is required in bent furniture parts, structural frames and has extra strength. It has creamy white or gray color to light brown. The grain of ash resembles that of oak.

Beech

It is also an inexpensive wood of pale color and is known for its bending ability. You can find it in the eastern half of the United States. Though it is not used in comparison to the ash, (most probably because it is not eye catching at all) but you can make furniture pieces that are not the center of attraction or are placed in hidden places. For instance, drawer bottoms or back and sides of the cabinets.

It goes well with stains and is stained like mahogany, cherry or maple. It is not suitable to use the hand tools due to its hardness.

Hickory

There are 15 species of hickory grown in the eastern United States.8 of them are important and used for commercial purposes.

Moderately priced, hard and tough Hickory is the best choice for lawn furniture, rockers, Windsor chairs and veneers. This hardwood has brown o reddish brown color and is heavy. Hand tools are not suitable to work with. It is closed grained and do not have many figures.

Elm

Elm is quite expensive due to its excellent bending properties. It is rarely found as the trees were destroyed by Dutch elm disease. It is light brown to dark brown with streaks of red in it. It is suitable for both office and home furniture. Restaurant owners do not hesitate to use it for the furniture even if it is to be placed outdoors.

Birch

Birch is found in northeast US and Canada. People love this light brown timber with a yellowish tinge due to its attractive grain pattern. It is heavy and hard used for almost wide range of furniture and doors. It is also used for floors and cabinets. The only drawback is its cost. Birch is moderately expensive hardwood.

SOFTWOODS

Pine

More than 100 species of pine are found throughout the world. It is grown in the Northern hemisphere.

Properties

Its color is pale yellow and is lightweight hence easy to move. It is a soft wood that do not swell or shrink. It lacks figure and is straight grained.

Uses

Pine with knots is used for decorative wooden pieces. It is also used for provincial and country furniture. Although it is not long lasting, but its price makes it affordable and popular among masses. It needs a primer for an even finish and application should be before staining. You can use it to make wooden box to keep jewelry or other valuables.

Cedar

This durable and beautiful wood is excellent for making cabinets or the inner lining of cabinets. It has a pleasant aroma and has the quality to repel moths.

It is a renowned light weight wood having fine grain. Cedar is able to withstand harsh climatic changes. You need to avoid staining or bleaching cedar.

Redwood

Amazing fact about redwood is that its trees age is 2,500 years and they grow up to 300 feet tall. Grown in Pacific United States, it is considered to be best for outdoor furniture due to its characteristic of resistance to weather effects like moisture, sunlight and bugs. It has deep reddish brown color and has growth rings on it. You can manage redwood with hand tools and its cost varies region to region.

Spruce

It is softwood that is hard but light in weight. It is used for making boxes, crates, ladders and general millworks. It can shrink and has less resistance to wear and tear process.

Fir

You can use it for a variety of furniture making projects like doors, plywood, windows, veneer, frames and millwork. Brown and golden color can be enhanced by using stain. This versatile wood is not a strong resistant towards decay.

Hemlock

Hemlock has a uniform texture and is very light in weight. Its property if accepting glue and gripping screws makes it acceptable for all types of furniture. It is also used for the construction purpose like sub flooring and paneling. It can be used for making crates, doors, boards and planks. Both hand tools and power tools are easy to use with this wood. Its strength and resistance to wear and tear makes it popular for making cabinets, window frames and ladders. Western species of Hemlock is more liked as compared to the eastern one due to its resin free quality. It gives smooth finish and accepts any kind of stain.

TOOL SHOP

Among the first things any start woodworker should do is put up a marathon. Like so many different things a beginner woodworker have to perform, the groundwork of marathon contours the abilities and enjoyment of this craft long following the newcomer is getting an advanced woodworker. Tool storage alternatives are generally totally inadequate for the exceptional demands of hand tools along with their handy use. The overall absence of concern for the distinctive needs of hand instrument use conspires to restrict the capacity of any prospective hand instrument craftsman. Unlike contemporary stores where every new tool buy calls for a corresponding extra allotment of floor area after some necessary hand tool function places are created, there is seldom a need for any further expansion. The secret is getting these regions laid out in this manner; they don't stop your potential success.

ROOM TO PLANE

A workbench can be utilized for hand planing and a slew of joinery surgeries. You cannot create 8'-extended passes over inventory resting to a 6' seat. Crosscutting the inventory before moulding has disadvantages.

A sheet of the scrap put between your inventory and the wall gives a handy backstop for the substance being planed. The walls also prevent resources from being pumped off the trunk and supplies a handy place to get a chisel rack as well as other instrument storage. An anti-fatigue mat facing your seat is much more than just a luxury. Plane shavings can create finished concrete or wood floors quite slippery, even when they have been floated away. Planing extended inventory requires quite a little foot function, so I advise considering a sweepable non-refundable workout mat of some type.

SPACE TO SAW

Learning to watch by hand provides woodworkers with the chance to explore traditional joinery. Like whatever else attempts to find out, it is simpler to watch great tools and the ideal space. In Anglo-American stores, ripping is done sawhorses employing a wide-bladed "western" saw. The dimensions and shape are necessary for ripping matches nicely right adjacent to the seat. I believe this consequent 4' × 11' rectangle will be the minimum size to the most fabulous hand instrument store. One benefit of working hardwood with hand tools will be you can operate extensive inventory that could be too heavy or hard to muscular throughout machines. Having room to tear directly facing your workbench prevents you from needing to take some vast boards by your store. Nevertheless, if space is so tight, it is possible to tear almost everywhere. It's rather simple to take your sawhorses out and tear in the patio or at the backyard.

Anglo-American woodworkers got off with tail vices for 100 decades and so will you. You should not leave space to the best of your seat for your offcut. A very long offcut isn't simple to support here anyhow.

TOOL STORAGE SPACE

Employed tools are not like hand-held tools. Dropping them is usually catastrophic. Metal tools are more sensitive to rust, and which may result in pits in glossy metallic blades. Wooden tools are also sensitive to fluctuations in humidity. Finding effective methods of saving hand tools has been the attempt of craftsmen for decades. As opposed to suggesting a radical solution created of medium-density fiberboard, a fast glance back at what's been done may be wise.

Pictures of pre-industrial stores clearly show a two-pronged method of storing gear. Oft-used gears, generically known as "seat tools" for the ever-present place on the seat, are displayed kept on open shelves, or hung from hooks on the walls. Tool chests often painted a blue, green color (possibly because the copper-based pigment has been cheap), are revealed in many pictures of pre-industrial stores. For several years I thought that these bows were only a convenient way of hauling a journeyman's applications since he "journeyed" from store to shop. I was incorrect. These chests are large and remarkably heavy. Along with the word "journeyman" is the English corruption of the French phrase for "work "(Journee) speaking to not the travelling character of this employee but instead how he is paid for his job (to get a day's work).

These are a remarkably effective means to store hand tools. Tools can easily be obtained, protected from the dangers of this workshop, movable (with some trouble) and the torso is discreet. Made properly, the torso's tight-fitting lids appear to guard the contents against rust. Popular Woodworking has provided several strategies for instrument chests and walk-in closets. One benefit of a conventional tool chest is it may be emptied seasonally if needed. If we specify the "seat tools" correctly and as these tools used nearly always, rust shouldn't be an issue. However, fantastic changes in temperature or humidity need us to rethink the entire notion of chair gear. An excellent tool chest can make a superb window chair or table. Tool chests in the 18th century have been usually identical from blanket chests. Why don't you place one in your bedroom? Tools necessary to get a day's job may be unpacked and hung on walls or put on open shelves just to be returned after an evening's job without a fantastic loss in efficacy and a few substantial gain in reassurance.

LUMBER STORAGE SPACE

Planing and sawing by hand compel you to browse the grain, and also feel its motion, variations in density, etc... I am none of those men and women who fall in love with timber or its grain. However, a comprehensive familiarity with this material is inevitable. Before too long, each hand instrument user develops tastes for specific timber species, air-dried inventory instead of kiln cooked or dried, as well as particular cuts of timber like quarter sawn, plainsawn heart timber, flitches, etc. Therefore, and undoubtedly, the other hand tool users that I understand buy wood which meets their tastes regardless of if they have an immediate use for this or not. I think it's wise if at all possible, to get ready for the long term storage of a fantastic amount of timber for future endeavors. Nonetheless, your timber rack should not automatically share your workspace. You might locate your garage, woodshed, or possibly a shady part of your yard or backyard a suitable place for your timber rack. When designing your timber rack, think about such matters as providing adequate airflow through the stands, availability and shading the timber from the sun. If children are part of your daily life, please take every precaution to make your lumber stand safe for somebody who can confuse it for a jungle gym.

SHARPENING SPACE

It's been stated that the real key to working together with hand tools is learning how to reconstruct them. No supreme hand tool store is complete with no provisions such as sharpening. Even though Jacques-Andre Robe's 18thcentury text reveals an active sharpening region, and this is not an absolute requirement. The workbench may be a handy spot to sharpen since its sturdy and just the ideal height for this kind of action. However, there are many reasons why many favor a dedicated place since Robot illustrated. Most sharpening gear demands some type of lubrication, which may make a wreck of your seat and some other future jobs. Grinders utilized by some woodworkers spew nasty abrasive particle dust. Let us face it. Sharpening is a dirty business. If the distance is short, contemplate some type of mat to secure your seat from water or oil which may fly off the finish of your stone. This rubber mat works dual duty. It shields the seat and retains the rock from falling around. For mild emitting, your seat may indeed deteriorate; however, if more severe work is necessary, it is beautiful to have a committed sharpening region. A grinder plus a tiny shop-built table with a suitable height will suit the bill.

The sharpening station should not always maintain the workshop. It might be at an unheated or undesirable site. However, an inconvenient sharpening area can dissuade you from waxing. Nothing will dissuade a woodworker quicker or more thoroughly than functioning with boring tools. At the "supreme" marathon, there could be a few well-equipped waxing areas. The rest of us only have to discover a distance we could make a mess inside.

LIGHTING YOUR WORKSPACE

Within an article I wrote about the Anthony Hay cabinet shop at Colonial Williamsburg, master cabinetmaker Mack Headley clarified a number of the advantages of operating at "raking" mild. The organic light out of a nearby window throws shadows, so letting him see a surface if planing or dividing. I've discovered knife outlines to be invisible under the shadow-less flooding of light out of 4'-fluorescent shop lights. Shortly after that trip Colonial Williamsburg eliminated the 4' store lights on my seat and started experimenting with various sorts of lighting.

Here is what I ended up. Lighting the endings of the seat is crucial. Even though it's counter-intuitive, the capacity to turn lights off separately can assist you to see what you want to view. Within my seat I am using a range of 13-watt, compact fluorescent bulbs at clamp work lighting fittings (they have a colour temperature of 3,500K). These bulbs discard incredible white lighting, are cheap, and, most significant, may be turned off separately or immediately repositioned, providing me slopes where and when I want them. I made sure to place lighting within the ends of the seat where the best work is finished. You can substitute conventional incandescent bulbs at comparable fixtures or pick the much warmer as well as brighter halogens, but those might require exceptional fixtures. I discovered higher-colour temperature compact fluorescent (CF) bulbs supplied better lighting compared to lower-color CF bulbs using double the wattage. Together with all the raking light switched and the over-bench lights turned off, I could quickly see if I want to sharpen my eloquent plane.

AN INVITING SHOP

By far among the most refreshing things relating to the best hand tool store is that using a few precautions, and it could be made secure enough to get a baby. Woodworking is this a solitary hobby, but it should not be. With no sound and the dust of machines, the store may be a nice place to be. My store has toys for your kids (though they favor tenon cheeks and plane shavings) plus a cosy spot to sit. The wood paneling did not take long to put in, but it took off the harshness of their cinderblock walls. The most magnificent store is a store that you are interested in being in. The most magnificent store is a store where a child or grandchild, spouse or partner feels welcome. The most magnificent store is a store where woodworking could be shared.

TOOL MAINTENANCE

Keeping care of one's tools is an important practice for many reasons, primarily concerning the safety and well-being of the tool's owner, though it is also of great importance to allow your tools to keep cutting wood for as long as possible. Different tools require different degrees of care, and that depends almost entirely on the amount of moving parts, and the types of blades. Sometimes it can be as simple as talking something to a grindstone on occasion, though other times, maintaining sharpness can be a real pain. With other tools, it requires ensuring that power tools are continuing to cut or drill straight and are true in their precision.

Many tools, even simple handsaws or a screwdriver bit set, come with a small booklet that outlines how to keep and maintain them. Due to the wide variety of tools available, this guide will be unable to go into the specifics of every model and brand of every tool, but instead, this will provide general tips on how to care for and maintain such tools. Even so, keeping a hold of these small booklets can help you with a niche problem you may experience to that tool.

Using the tools the way they were meant to be used is essential to not only maintaining their long-term usefulness, but also to keeping the tool's user safe and secure throughout the tools continued use. If a tool is misused, it is not only dangerous, but often voids the tool's warranty, assuming it had a warranty.

HANDSAW MAINTENANCE

Keeping handsaws sharp can seem a daunting task, but in all honestly, it's a matter of proper habits and common sense. Firstly, as with all metal tools, one should store saws in a dry, moisture-free environment, such as a toolbox or tool chest. Charcoal or silica packets can help keep enclosed spaces such as those free of moisture, and this will keep your saws from rusting. Another way to keep rust off of your saw-blades is to spray them with WD-40 after you've finished using them, and there's no need to dry it off after application.

If your saws have wooden handles, using oils to keep them from drying or cracking in these moisture-free environments will ensure you won't need to replace the handles any time soon. A boiled linseed oil is recommended, though there are alternatives that can also be used, such as orange oil or Tung oil. If rust has already accumulated, use razor blades and 320 grit sandpaper to clean it off, always moving along the length of the saw, away from the handle. Never remove rust moving widthwise on the saw, meaning don't go from spine to blade, always move from "heel", or the start of the handle, to the "toe", or the flat end-side of the saw, which is across from the heel, and never sand or razor towards yourself.

Keeping the handle of a handsaw in good condition is important to ensuring you can trust in every push out and pull inwards, without the handle shattering mid-cut. We've already gone over keeping it maintained with oils, but sometimes, while secured to the blade, it can accumulate built-up rust, which reduces its strength. To clean rust off a handle, simply remove it from the saw and apply a razor blade or sandpaper of a smaller grit to it, carefully cutting away at only the rusted holes that secure the handle to the saw. Apply oil to it, drying it off afterwards, and reattach it to the blade.

HAND TOOL MAINTENANCE

Hand tools are an important thing to maintain. Though are only ever used for precision work, keeping tools in good condition ensure that such work remains precise, instead of losing its edge due to poor keepings. Hammers, saws, wedges, and small cutting or whittling instruments should not be allowed to remain unprotected outside of use. Store them as soon as possible, in a well-controlled environment. Sharpening any hand tools that require it, such as planes or wedges, can be done normally, usually with a grindstone of some kind. If the handles begin to wear away, consider replacing the tool if it is inexpensive or repairing/replacing the handle if it is a costly tool.

DRILL PRESS MAINTENANCE

Drill presses are more complex than they seem, though despite this, maintaining them is not a difficult task. To keep a drill press working smoothly, there are many things that need to be done, though they are all relatively simple.

Firstly, lubricating the chuck, which are the closing jaws that grasp the bit, is essential to ensuring that they can close securely around the bit. Empty the chuck and open the jaws fully. Blow out any dust or wood chips with a puff of pressurized air, wearing goggles to ensure nothing gets in your eyes. Look into the chuck to make certain it is clear before proceeding. After it is emptied of all excess material, spray small amounts of lubricant up and into the chuck, moving the jaws of the chuck as you spray. The excess lubricant will drop out, leaving you with a smoothly turning grasping system. Polish off any remaining lubricant, and you're good to go.

After this is done, another good point of inspection is the power cord. Ensure that the cord is secured tightly on both the machine-side and the socket-side, and check for any cracks, cuts, or openings in the cord itself. If any are present, consider repairing the cord with a rubber sealant, or replacing it altogether.

To further ensure your drill press is in optimal working order, one needs to ensure that their drill is drilling true. There are several factors that can impact the straightness at which a drill tunnels, the simplest of which is the angle at which the bit is inserted, which should always be as close to 90 degrees as possible; to the most complex, which is a press which is misaligned. Even the latter is an issue that can be solved at home, however. The first thing to check, after ensuring the bit has been properly inserted, is to make certain your drill is correctly set up. If your press is tilted slightly in its setup, it can affect the straightness at which it drills.

BAND SAW MAINTENANCE

The first thing to know about band saw maintenance right off the bat is the necessity to "break in" blades. Breaking in the blade of a band saw will allow it to remain sharper for much longer. When purchased new, band saw blades are far too sharp for normal use, and will chip and break at microscopic levels if not properly broken in. The solution is to cut slower for the first 50 inches of use. Cutting slower does not imply reducing band saw blade running speed, the blade should always run at the same cutting speed, but instead, means to feed the wood in slower, about half as fast as one normally would. You don't have to measure out exactly how long every single cut you make is but try and maintain the first 50 inches at half pressure. If you're unsure about the amount of pressure that should be used, experiment cautiously and move wood through at a slow pace. Eventually, as you continue to break in the blade, you will understand the normal rate of cutting, and how you should cut when breaking in a new blade.

Regularly clean your band saw's bench and blade. Keeping the bench free of sawdust and rust is recommended, simply sweep off sawdust with a wire brush, and remove rust using a razor or chemical cleaners. To clean the blade, power off the machine and remove the band saw's plastic side cover, taking the band from between its housing in the wheels. You can polish the blade using a combination of resin removers and cotton cloth. This will keep the blade from getting caked with resin, which would sit on the blade and potentially cause it to shake or bound around in its housing, which could directly damage your machine. While the blade is out of its housing, you can apply the same resin remover to clean the wheels as you did the blade. Soaking the blade in a soapy solution for cleaning is also acceptable, as long as you take care not to let it rust.

SANDING TOOL MAINTENANCE

Handheld sanding tools operate in much the same way most power tools do, though there is much to be said about belt sander maintenance. The first and most obvious tip for maintaining your belt sander is the regular upkeep of the band of sandpaper itself. They typically last long when properly applied, and this means not pressing too hard into the tool as you sand. You can use a good deal of force, but do not stretch or warp the sandpaper as you work. Keep the motor free of sawdust as best as you can, and regularly empty the sawdust collection bin affixed to most belt sanders. If your belt sander has come affixed with a vacuum tube, one should run a shop vac through the tube during the operation of the belt sander.

POWER TOOL GENERAL MAINTENANCE

Power tools are, in general, very similar motor setups that can be cared for in the same ways. A few symptoms of worn or well-used power tools can be repaired easily, while others will require a professional touch.

Power tools use brushes, solid blocks of carbon, to help them conduct electricity to the motor. These wear out over time, and you can tell when they're getting worn when you can start to see visible but harmless sparks inside your power tool during regular sustained use. In most modern power tools, the brushes can be easily replaced, and one can tell if this is the case for their tool by identifying two black covers on opposite sides of the motor housing, called the brush caps. If these are present on your tool, replacing the brushes is as simple as ordering a new pair from your tool's manufacturer, and removing the caps and brushes, before replacing them. Be warned that as you loosen the brush caps, the springs loaded into the brushes might cause the cap to shoot loose, so be ready for it by pressing a finger into the cap as you unscrew it, and gingerly removing it.

If your power tools have removable blades, unslot your blades before storing to store them in a separate, moisture-controlled environment. Doing this will help keep your blades rust-free, and will keep the actual tool itself from locking itself onto the blade, and will ensure that you can easily remove or replace the blade in the future.

Keeping the air vents clean with quick bursts of pressurized air will also help your power tool running smoothly and efficiently for long periods of time. Be careful not to maintain a constant spray as you do this, due to the nature of pressurized air cans. Using quick bursts and occasionally revving the motor to move it about will help you achieve a cleaner motor.

Look into screws and fasteners that are securing the casing of your tool, as they might have been shaken loose by the power of the tool itself. Tighten screws regularly, and if you can't identify or don't own a screwdriver with the correct head, take your tool into a hardware store and ask an employee about purchasing a screwdriver or drill bit that matches that specific type of screw.

Two things that always go hand-in-hand are the maintenance of tools, and the safe use of them. Using tools safely is the ultimate tip on how to maintain them, though the safe use of tools is a complex enough.

SAFETY WHILE WOODWORKING

Since working with wood possesses a high risk for injury due to the combination of sharp tools and strength involved. Safety when woodworking mainly involves common sense, but is often overlooked. It may be because of the predominantly lax demeanor of the majority of woodworkers or their mentality of "it will not happen to me."

Below are the 10 most basic yet important rules for safety when working with wood:

DO NOT FORGET TO WEAR THE NEEDED SAFETY EQUIPMENT

First and foremost, it is imperative for the individual to get a hold of the needed safety equipment. There is a number of basic safety equipment every woodworker must have and wear when performing their tasks:

Safety Glasses

The eyes are very delicate structures that serve a multitude of vital functions – the most basic of which is sight. The mere introduction of a foreign substance into these structures will cause irritation, redness and inflammation. Sometimes it is painful. When something more harmful enters into these structures or when debris plummet into the eyes at a high speed and acceleration, some semi-permanent or even completely permanent damage may be dealt.

When woodworking, a lot of dust or debris fly around, especially when using power tools. Wearing a good pair of impact resistant lenses that completely cover the eyes without hindering vision could make all the difference. These usually appear as transparent goggles with side screens.

Hearing Protection

More often than not, woodworking involves the use of very noisy equipment that, aside from being irritating to the ears, may cause hearing damage. Some commonly used examples are surface planner and routers.

There are two basic types of hearing protection devices: ear muffs and ear plugs. The former is said to provide a greater degree of protection from the noise, but may become a bit of a hassle to use.

Using any of these devices when working with all these noisy equipment's will aid the user in decreasing susceptibility to long term hearing loss.

Latex Gloves

There are also a lot of chemicals involved, like when finishing a piece. These substances may bore through the skin and

Face Shield

There are also circumstances where wood chips fly all over the place. Albeit being small, getting hit by these is far from a pleasant experience as they fly at high speeds. As a supplement to the eye shield, use a face shield to protect a greater area of the face.

Face Masks and Respirators

A good number of woodworking tools generate a lot of dust and wood shavings. These tiny particles can be breathed in and may cause respiratory problems. Therefore, one must always wear a face mask when working.

There are also a lot of odorous chemicals involved, such as varnish and paint. Breathing in these strong odors may also cause some respiratory problems and, if there are fumes produced, may cause damage to the lungs. In such cases, a respirator is recommended.

DO NOT DRINK WHILE WORKING

This type of job requires a high level of concentration and a keen eye on detail. Drinking alcohol while on the job will only impair your thinking or decrease your attention span. This is a dangerous mix.

Do have self-control and only drink after the job is done.

UNPLUG EQUIPMENT BEFORE CHANGING BLADES

There are many types and sizes of blades used in woodworking, each with a specific purpose. Most certainly, the time when these blades need to be changed will definitely arrive. When doing so, it is imperative to unplug the equipment prior to changing the blade. This means that one has to go to the trouble of disconnecting the tool from the power source itself and not just click the off switch. Many woodworkers who have forgotten this rule or ho have chosen to ignore it completely have lost a digit or two because of this. Some have even received worse injuries.

AS MUCH AS POSSIBLE, USE ONLY A SINGLE EXTENSION CORD

Most tools to be used require the use of electricity or some sort of power source. It is for this reason that many woodworkers find themselves entangled in a mess of wires halfway through the job. Using only a single, heavy duty extension wire for all power tools with the same voltage will help keep the area nice and tidy.

A more important reason for using only a single extension cord for tools with similar voltages is in connection to the previous safety rule. If only a single extension wire is used, the woodworker will be forced to switch the wire for every piece of equipment before the tool could be utilized. This serves as a reminder for one to plug and unplug the equipment when swapping tools and it will make a good habit when switching blades as the user is more mindful of fully turning off the equipment when making adjustments.

In a way, it is a form of self-discipline.

DO NOT USE DULL BLADES AND BITS

Using sharp, clean of pitch, and well cared for equipment does not only make the job much easier, the cut cleaner, and the final output of a considerably higher quality, it is also an important element of safety.

It is especially dangerous to use rusty equipment as these devices are not only brittle or may break easily when exposed to high levels of pressure or force, these pieces of equipment may also cause serious health problems when they cut through the user's flesh. There is a high chance of catching tetanus or having the wound get infected if the user is cut with a rust tool.

There is also increased effort and workload with dull tools and the woodworker will have to exert extra effort in cutting up or carving the blocks of wood.

DO NOT FORGET TO CHECK FOR METALLIC DEBRIS

Since there is a high degree of detail that is involved in this rather physical job, it is imperative for one to check and double check every step of the way. It may be tiring and very meticulous, but the results produced will be worth the extra dose of effort.

Be sure to always check up on the presence of tiny metallic debris like screws, nails, and the like in the piece of wood to be cut or worked on prior to cutting it up. This is a safety precaution. If metallic debris hits or is cut by a fast moving sharp power tool, there is a high change that the debris will fly into the air and cause a far greater degree of damage to the user than any chip of wood could make.

Remember, prevention is always better than cure.

There is no cure for a lost limb. That part shall forever remain lost and the scar it shall create shall forever serve as a reminder to stay safe and observe the rules of safety when working a high risk job that involves the use of sharp equipment.

WORK AGAINST THE CUTTER

Electrically powered cutting equipment for wood are designed to slice in the opposite direction of the movement of the wood. When cutting a stock of the material, be sure to incise into it and not with it.

KEEP A SAFE DISTANCE FROM MOVING BLADES

Working with sharp tools always poses a risk for danger – especially with heavy duty apparatus. To keep all limbs intact and complete, always wait until the blades have come to a full stop before going anywhere near them. Moreover, there are instances where the switches malfunction or are unintentionally and unknowingly bumped, which may set off the device again. That is why it is best to take precautionary measures. To remove cut-offs from the razor, use a stick to poke the waste material off.

STAY FOCUSED

Selective sustained attention refers to a person's capability of intentionally staying focused on a task consistently. It has been said that the average adult could sustain this said concentration for approximately 10 minutes and cannot last for more than 40 minutes at a time. However, this varies from person to person. Take this into consideration and make sure to work at set amounts of time before taking a short breaker to make sure that there are no distractions during work. Not focusing on the work is a recipe for disaster.

WEAR THE PROPER ATTIRE

In order for one to eliminate or at least diminish the risk for injury or danger, one must dress appropriately. This means that there should be no loose articles of clothing, dangling earrings, necklaces, or anything that may get caught up or entangled in the equipment.

The woodworker must wear comfortable clothes as this type of work requires a good amount of time to perform and finish. These clothes must fit properly and snugly. One must wear a long sleeved shirt and, if the hair is long, have it tied back or kept. Long pants also provide sufficient protection.

There are times when the need for a shop apron to provide an extra layer of protection arises – particularly when one is using a lathe. As for footwear, these must be steel-toed work shoes. Do not, by all means, expose the feet or leave them unprotected.

SANDING AND FINISHING

For many woodworkers in the middle of a project, a good part of the excitement seems to vanish once the dovetail saw and the chisels, or the router and the band saw, have done their work. At that point, few of us can muster great enthusiasm for the work that lies ahead—sanding, staining, and finishing.

This is understandable. Sanding and finishing don't provide the immediate gratification that comes from seeing pieces of wood change form and join other pieces to become something entirely new. And the process of finishing, particularly sanding, can take some pretty hard work. But if you decide to cut corners so close to the end—at the finish line, as it were—you're only cheating yourself. It may seem like a good idea now to skip that one pass with another grit of sandpaper, or not to rub out the finish yet one more time. But thorough sanding and a good finish are what make the difference between a great piece of work and one that is merely adequate, and between one that will be treasured for years to come and one that will require refinishing before you know it.

SANDING MATERIALS

When you're finishing a woodworking project, you start and end with sandpaper. Although the serious sanding takes place before you apply your first coat of finish, you still need to use some elbow grease to buff and shine even after your final coat has been applied.

If you plan to stain the wood, you need to sand it first to prepare the wood surface. When sanding, be sure to remove all wood fibers and open up the wood grain; this will ensure a penetrating, uniform finish.

This preparation process also includes removing any other serious defects you see, such as grease or indentations. If you don't have a clean, smooth surface to work with, the stain and the finish won't sink into the wood pores evenly.

When you reach the staining phase, the penetration of your chosen stain in a hardwood will ultimately depend on the final grit you used to sand the wood. Grits range from 12, which is extremely coarse, to 1,500, which is incredibly fine. You are not likely to use either of those grits, though, as woodworkers generally use from 40 to 600 grit.

In the process of sanding, you will be "working through the grits." This means that you start with a rougher sandpaper (lower grit number) and work your way up through a series of progressively smoother grades (higher grit number) to a final finish. At each step, the smoother sandpaper removes the marks left by the lower grade and leaves some of its own. In general, the progression of sandpaper grits is as follows: 40 to

60—Coarse: Heavy sanding; stripping off paint or other finishes; roughing up the surface.

You can use 40- to 50-grit sandpaper for smoothing very rough wood surfaces, though for wood that is reasonably smooth you are better off starting with a medium grit. Before applying any stain or finish, most woodworkers sand using up to a 180 grit, and some use up to 200 or 220 grit. Depending on what type of finish you are applying, the entire finishing process may take you up to a 400 or even a 600 grit.

Don't panic: you don't need to hit every stop along the way in your progression—that would make for truly endless sanding. But for a clear and smooth finish, you will need to employ a minimum of three (and more likely four to six) different grits.

When moving through your grit sequence, try not to skip more than one grit number. This will lengthen the life of your sandpaper and whatever implement you're using to engage it, and it will give you a higher-quality finish.

The back row is a sampling of sanding disks. In front, from left, sanding papers of these varieties: silicon carbide wet/dry; garnet; and aluminum oxide.

After your wood has been sanded and cleaned, you might want to test your work. Before beginning the coloring process, sponge the surface of the wood with water, alcohol, or any solvent to reveal any areas that might contain glue, marks, or any uneven sanding.

TYPES OF SANDPAPER

Sandpaper comes in several types, which are manufactured for specific uses. These include the following:

Aluminum oxide: This manufactured sandpaper usually comes in an off-brown color and is incredibly abrasive. Woodworkers use it mostly for stripping old paint or varnish or for finishing hardwoods. It's also used for finishing some metals.

Emery sandpaper: Emery is a natural abrasive, black in color, and is most often used for lightly polishing metals.

Garnet sandpaper: Garnet is a natural sandpaper, as well, and while it is not quite as abrasive as manufactured sandpapers, it's made a bit tougher from heat treating. Garnet is popular with woodworkers for finish-sanding fine hardwood furniture projects.

Silicon carbide: This manufactured sandpaper is most often black in color and is the hardest of the commonly used abrasives. It's used for hand-sanding both softwood and hardwood projects.

Zirconia alumina: This manufactured sandpaper is most often used for heavy sanding, such as with a belt sander.

DYES, STAINS, AND FILLERS

Dyes are basically a mixture of colorants in mineral spirits, oil, alcohol, or water. A dye will change the hue of your wood without concealing its figure. Dyes penetrate both soft and hard grains. Dye particles have smaller molecular structures than the mineral particles found in stains. This is why dyes appear to be more transparent. Dyes also bind to wood naturally and therefore don't require an additional binder.

Stains are created from a variety of sources, ranging from synthetic materials to organic minerals. Stains consist of finely ground pigment particles that are suspended, or dispersed, in either a water-based or oil-based solvent. After the stain is applied, the solvent evaporates, leaving the color on the wood. Pigments are pretty easy to use and come in a wide variety of colors that can be added to other stains to increase color and/or density.

Many woodworkers will color their wood project with a dye, then stain it, in order to avoid covering the grain of the wood with the saturation of a dark color. Dyes seem to stain the grain and the areas between the grains about the same color, whereas pigmented stains seem to fill the grain, leaving the wood surface with a little less color.

FILLERS, SEALERS, AND GLAZES

You must then seal everything with a sealer. Some top-coat finishes are self-sealing, or you may need to apply the sealer separately. Often, vinyl sealers are used to lock in the color and protect the grain.

The sealer performs many functions: It locks in the color, seals the grain, begins the filling process, and gives you a coating you can sand.

Glazes are applied after the sealer. These are transparent stains that are used to even out a light and dark area, as you see the true color of wood only after the sealer has been sanded. Tinted applications of a sealer or top coat, called toners, can also be used to intensify color.

FINISHES

Top coats come in a variety of forms, from shellacs to polyurethanes. Each form has different preparation techniques and characteristics that you should keep in mind when making your choice.

- Danish oil is easy to use, but it dries very slowly. Amber in color, Danish oil dries to a satin finish and has low moisture resistance.

- Lacquer dries quickly and is clear. It is highly glossy, durable, and resistant to moisture.

- Polyurethane is another slow drier and comes in gloss, semi gloss, and satin. Colors range from clear to amber. Polyurethane is incredibly durable and moisture resistant.

- Shellac is an economical, high-gloss, and quick-drying option with color choices ranging from amber to clear. It comes in liquid form, as do all other top coats. It's affected by water, alcohol, and heat, so it is best for indoor projects.

- Tung oil is easy to apply as it requires no mixing and comes ready to use, although it does dry slowly. Satin in appearance, tung oil isn't very resistant to moisture.

- Varnish takes much longer to dry than lacquer and comes in gloss, semigloss, or satin. Amber in color, varnish is durable and resistant to moisture.

THE DURABILITY OF FINISHES, INDOORS AND OUT

The toughest challenge to a finish is, naturally, exposure to the elements. For outdoor furniture, this may include rain, snow, extreme temperature changes, and more. Even so, the failure of exterior finishes is usually the result of the wrong kind of finish being applied to the wood surface or of not following recommended application procedures.

Each wood variety has unique characteristics that will affect the durability of any finish applied to it.

EASY BEGINNERS' PROJECTS

Woodworking is a great hobby and a vocation that can last a lifetime. The following are woodworking projects and can be used by woodworkers of all ages. Some projects include plans and a list of resources and equipment, so you have all you need to proceed.

A CHAIR

This design is based loosely on an Adirondack chair, but in its structure, it is much simpler. This chair can be made with just two 1-inch x 10-inch x 10-foot pieces of wood, and it should take only a few hours.

A CHAIR

Materials:

Round saw / rafter sq.m / bar clamps / roundless drill / two 1"x 10"x 10' cedar boards or other weather-resistant wood tissue / 48 1/2 "outer wood quality content Collection• 2 Seatback 9¼"x 32 "• 2 Seat 9¼"x 20¼ "• 1 front stretcher / 5½"x 21¾ "(belted 30 degrees around one rim) Instead you develop subassemblies to create the platform.

To make the shorter bits, tear the entire board in one move and then cut parts to length is more effective. But cut off a 25¾ "full-width piece before you do. It's not half ripped; later.

Steps:

1. Rip down the middle of the rest of the piece, so you are a little under 45⁄8 inches wide with two boards. Use the other 10-foot board as a guide to keep your cut line straight. Apply this guide to the board so that the base plate of your saw runs along the bottom of the manual, and the blade slices through the center of the surface. For most saws, this means that the guide is 11⁄2 inches away. Add a few screws to the guide; you can remove the holes later.

2. Cut all 14 sections from the two 1x ten panels to length by a circular saw, according to the cut list. You're not going to have many scraps— just enough to build a bonfire.

3. Take the piece of the first board and cut it to 30% inches. Clamp one of the armrests to the wall if you need a map. The more significant part is the front stretcher, and the other half is the backrest.

4. Label a 20-degree cut on each rear-leg blank in the front section. Place the rafter square pivot point on the top corner of the leg and move the rafter to the side of the board in the clockwise direction. Cut the line. Cut. Cut a 3x1-inch rectangle off the lower corner on the back of your hip. Build two bracelets with a single tear. Label the side, lock the blank on to a work surface and cut it carefully.

5. Clamping the tapered arm to the front legs and adding armrests to the front and inner front legs, overhanging them 3⁄4 inch. Push into each front leg two screws and one arm brace. Attach the backrest, side up, to the pair. Hold square assembly. Drive a few screws through each arm and backrest, taking care not to break the workpiece. Install the seatbacks by driving two torches across each leg and three lights into the backrest and backrest. Don't go too hard or punch yourself across the other leg.

6. Assemble: This chair can be built from only two 1-inch x 10-inch x 10-foot pieces of wood, and it should only take a couple of days.

7. Start the chair by trimming the outside corners of the frame. It ought to feel like that.

8. Put the end of the wood on the ground and keep the other at the eye level to test for limits, crooks and twists. Open one eye and look for warping through the board. You can get away with somewhat deformed boards when you cut the lumber into smaller pieces. If not, stop something 1⁄2 inch or more bent over a 10-foot range.

WOODEN TOYS

The best children's gifts are handmade wooden toys, and if they look too sharp like this red wagon, they are forever appreciated. A toy car is the essential gift of a break, even in an environment as interactive as this. You don't need batteries, and you almost can't wear them out. This doesn't go out of style. The offspring will bring the dog around within a week. And if you design your car right, your children could use it one day for the same reason.

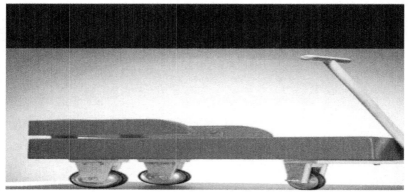

A WOODEN TOY CAR

Materials:

2x Side ¾"x 4½'x 24"

2x Bottom ¾"x 4½"x 14½"

1x Plywood bottom ½"x 16"x 24"

2x Side rail ¾"x 4½"x 12"

1x Back board ¾"x ¾"x 23⁄4 "I 2x Wheel mounting block ¾"x 13/4"x 33⁄4"x 1x Steering paddle ¾

Steps:

1) Make the wagon box sections and use the rubber first. Add wooden glue and 6d finishing nails to the front and back panels. Paint it all dark. Or any color. The best cars, though, are gold. Bore a 1/4-inch hole through the bottom panel for the steering bolt.

2) Make the rails, tracks and battens sideways. Mark the curve on the rails back and side. Cut curves with a puzzle and a 20-inch blade cut the curves. Clean these pieces and mark them. Once it is finished, add either bat on the side of the wagon and end with a pair of 1 "No. 6 wooden screws and finish washers.

3) Add Running Gear a right farm car is rolling on sturdy running gear and a right toy car is also running. Line the wheel trucks ' floorboard and solid wood blocks, then hold and pin them together. Attach a polyurethane layer on both ends. Stick the two rear wheel trucks onto the base panel and wait for the glue to cure before you move through the base panel and into the blocks of the wood with a pair of 3/4-inch screws with finishing launders.

4) Bring the handle on, cross the dowels, then put the short dowel in the direction and bore a hole with a spade bit into the middle of the handle. Add polyurethane to both dowels, and then hold to the longer dowel and screw it shorter.

Bore the pilot hole on the other side of the long dowel for an eye screw. Attach a large eye screw to a small eye screw to attach the handle to the cart. Turn the lower screw in the handle first and the bigger screw on the steering yok; then insert the bigger screw into the lower screw.

CHESSBOARD

Creating a chessboard is the one for the least amount of work out of all my woodworking tasks. You may assume it requires a repetitive process of cutting and pasting together 64 small squares of wood. This is a simple project, which only takes a few hours and takes a few days. You may even have all you need on hand.

Materials:

Saw (preferably table saw) bar clamps, Wood glue Orbital black framing square Slight and light wood (sufficient to make four twenty-four-inch strips, thick 3/4 "in each color) two types of hardness, like the oaks and mahogany. For the lighter wood, Maple is beautiful too. Mixing a smooth wood with hard wood like mahogany can hinder the sanding process later.

Steps:

1) Cut eight wooden strings, four of each tone. The strips will determine the distance by at least 20 inches (or whatever you choose for the square size). A table saw will give you the best chance for precision and accuracy. You can use a circular screw if necessary, but you want to set up a straight edge against which to drive the screw.

2) Place your strips in a different pattern (black, white, medium, red) once your pieces have been removed. Pick one hand for each one to be the top face (the one you'll see when the board is finished). If arranged in a way that you are comfortable with, I suggest numerating the strips which, if gluing begins, will be a useful reference guide.

3) Ensure that the adhesive is spread evenly throughout the edge of each string. It is essential that the gluing is done correctly, or items will break later.

4) The pins should be perpendicular to the board edges so that they don't make holes. Place bits of scrap timber between clamps and boards for the pressure transfer and safety of the curved side of the board when using soft wood, such as pines. When the strips are closed, clean the remaining adhesive with a damp rag from the top lip.

5) Furthermore, leave the surface as smooth as possible before gluing. The clamps typically curl up the edges,

producing a faint bowl appearance. When gluing and clamping, put a straight edge on the top of the board (sided and diagonal) and adjust it if needed. Any unevenness is all right; you'll sand it later. But now it's much better than later to live with it.

6) Cut Strips (again). Once the adhesive has dried, it is time to cut 2-inch strips off your recently made board. Render the cuts similar to the original stripes this time. Drag the squared-off side along the fence if you use a table saw because you started with 20-inch raw material lines, that leaves you with at least nine checkerboard strips. If one breaks or doesn't look right, there is an extra.

7) Sand the photo on the board. When the glue has cooled, smooth the surface, unclamp it.

8) Add a Border. To make it look nice, done, add a border. It can be as good as you want. Hold basic 3/4x1-inch strip of pine around the bottom. Make the' neck' of the bottom 1 inch wide, so the whole thing sits on the edge and not on the surface when it's on a table. It reflects the very slight bow that the board formed during the final adhesive. If required, sand the line.

9) Apply eventually, apply to your board whatever you want to end. You can also remove the border from the playing surface and use a Bar-top finish to make it look smoother.

Then you got it there. An hour here, an hour there, you've got a chessboard all of a sudden.

CONCLUSION

For beginners, woodworking might seem like a complex and hard task. However, once you make your first wood item, you'll realize that woodworking is quite easy. Here is a step by step guideline on how to build a woodwork product.

Step 1: Conceptualize.

Before you build any item, you must have an idea of what you want to build. Do you want to make a chair, table or wall unit? What kind of chair or table do you want to build? How big will the chair or table be? Where will you place the item you want to build? Are you building it for personal use or for commercial purposes? If you're building it for commercial purposes, do you have a ready market? If you have a ready market or if the item is preordered, you'll probably have limited time to finish the project.

Once you conceptualize and answer all the above questions, you'll figure out what is required so as to get started. If you're building something for personal use, you'll have all the time you need. You can also make any adjustment or alteration that you want if you're building an item for personal use.

Step 2: Visualize.

Once you have an idea of what you want to make, you should figure out how you want it to look like. This step involves figuring out specific details about the item you want to build. If you want to make a chopping board, what shape would you prefer? Do you want a rectangular or circular board? If you want to make a table, how will the top look like? How many legs will the table have?

Step 3: Create a layout or drawing of the item.

The third step involves creating a layout or drawing of the item you want to build. This stage is quite important as it will help you to think of parts that you had forgotten when visualizing. If you had forgotten to think of the support structures of the chair, you'll remember the parts once you draw them. At this stage you can consult other people and get their ideas about what you want to create. You can also make some modifications to the drawing.

So as to have a clear understanding of the item you want to build, you can create several drawings; each of them depicting the item from a different angle. You can use the drawing to come up with the exact size of the item that you want to build. If you're building a table, you can build a rectangular one whose top is measuring 3 x 4 feet. Once you know the exact measurements of the item you want to build, you can easily estimate the quantity of required materials.

Step 4: list different parts

The fourth step involves creating a list of the different parts of the item you want to build. You must also document the size of each of the listed parts. For instance, you may want to make a chair that is made of the top part (measuring 3 feet by 4 feet by 1 inch) and four legs (each one measuring 2.5 inch by 2.5 inch by 3 feet). A medium density fiberboard (MDF) may also be included as the top part of the table.

Step 5: List raw materials.

Now that you have a list of all the parts of the item you want to build, you can easily come up with a list of required raw materials. You should therefore go ahead and create a list of all the raw materials that you'll need. Make sure that you've included the quantity of each material that is required. Practical example of required raw materials may include nails, vanish, filler material and a piece of medium density fiber board.

Step 6: Acquire raw materials

Since you know what you need in order to get started, you can now purchase the raw materials. You should be very careful when purchasing raw materials so as to make sure that the project is completed successfully. For instance, you should buy stronger steel nails if you plan to use hardwood. When hammered, soft steel may bend instead of penetrating the hardwood. If you're planning to build an item that will be placed in the kitchen or bathroom, you should use hardwood instead of softwood. This is because hardwoods last longer than softwoods when placed in watery environments.

Step 7: Plan the project.

You now have to plan how you are going to implement the project. You have to think of how you'll start and how you plan to proceed. Which part will you begin with? For instance, you can decide that you'll start by making the four legs before making the top part of a table. You must also plan about when you plan to be through with the task. If possible create a schedule (work plan) and work hard towards achieving the stated objectives.

Step 8: Make sure you have all the tools.

This step involves checking the toolbox or workshop so as to make sure that you have all the tools that you'll need. If you want to make a chopping board, you should ensure that you have a saw, emery paper and tape measure.

Step 9: Start building different parts.

You can now start building each of the different parts of the item you want to build. For the case of the table, you can build the four legs before building the top part. You can decide to start with the smaller and hard to carve parts before making the large and easy to build parts.

Step 10: Assemble (join) the different parts.

After you've built each of the parts, you can go ahead and assemble them to form one whole unit. You should also use the filler material to fill all the dents in the finished product. Place the finished product in a cool and dry area for some time (a few hours) to allow the filler content to dry.

Step 11: Finishing.

You can now do the finishing. This includes sandpapering the item and removing the extra filler content. You must also ensure that the item is mechanically strong and can serve its purpose. If you're designing a chair, you must ensure that it can comfortably withstand an average adult sitting on it. To test its mechanical strength, hold it tight and try to shake it strongly. You can also sit on it while carrying extra weight so as to simulate a situation whereby a weighty individual will be sitting on it. If it remains intact, you can conclude that it is strong enough to serve its purpose.

Step 12: Painting.

The last step involves painting, varnishing or lacquering of the finished product. This step is very critical as it will determine the attractiveness of the end product. An attractive item will attract more money if you decide to sell it. If you're making the item for personal use, you can use varnish or paint that resembles the general theme in your home.

After following these steps, it will be easy for you to start building your first woodworking project either indoor or outdoor. Just don't forget that safety is more important that you have to consider in building your first wood project. Enjoy woodworking!

Printed in Great Britain
by Amazon